TREES AND OTHER POEMS

"Mine is no horse with wings, to gain
The region of the Spheral chime;
He does but drag a rumbling wain,
Cheered by the coupled bells of rhyme."

Coventry Patmore.

TREES
AND
OTHER POEMS

by

Joyce Kilmer

34501

New York

George H. Doran Company

TO
MY MOTHER

Gentlest of critics, does your memory hold
   (I know it does) a record of the days
   When I, a schoolboy, earned your generous praise
For halting verse and stories crudely told?
Over these childish scrawls the years have rolled,
   They might not know the world's unfriendly gaze;
   But still your smile shines down familiar ways,
Touches my words and turns their dross to gold.

More dear to-day than in that vanished time
   Comes your high praise to make me proud and strong.
In my poor notes you hear Love's splendid chime,
   So unto you does this, my work belong.
Take, then, a little gift of fragile rhyme:
   Your heart will change it to authentic song.

For permission to reprint these poems, I thank the editors of The Century Magazine, The London Spectator, The Catholic World, The Ave Maria, The Independent, The New York Times Review of Books, The New York Times Sunday Magazine, Harper's Weekly, The Bellman, The Smart Set, The Lyric Year, Collier's Weekly, The New World, The Churchman, and Poetry: A Magazine of Verse.

CONTENTS

CONTENTS

CONTENTS

THE TWELVE-FORTY-FIVE

(For Edward J. Wheeler)

WITHIN the Jersey City shed
    The engine coughs and shakes its head,
The smoke, a plume of red and white,
Waves madly in the face of night.
And now the grave incurious stars
Gleam on the groaning hurrying cars.
Against the kind and awful reign
Of darkness, this our angry train,
A noisy little rebel, pouts
Its brief defiance, flames and shouts—
And passes on, and leaves no trace.
For darkness holds its ancient place,
Serene and absolute, the king
Unchanged, of every living thing.
The houses lie obscure and still
In Rutherford and Carlton Hill.
Our lamps intensify the dark
Of slumbering Passaic Park.
And quiet holds the weary feet

THE TWELVE-FORTY-FIVE (continued)

That daily tramp through Prospect Street.
What though we clang and clank and roar
Through all Passaic's streets?   No door
Will open, not an eye will see
Who this loud vagabond may be.
Upon my crimson cushioned seat,
In manufactured light and heat,
I feel unnatural and mean.
Outside the towns are cool and clean;
Curtained awhile from sound and sight
They take God's gracious gift of night.
The stars are watchful over them.
On Clifton as on Bethlehem
The angels, leaning down the sky,
Shed peace and gentle dreams.   And I—
I ride, I blasphemously ride
Through all the silent countryside.
The engine's shriek, the headlight's glare,
Pollute the still nocturnal air.
The cottages of Lake View sigh
And sleeping, frown as we pass by.
Why, even strident Paterson
Rests quietly as any nun.

THE TWELVE-FORTY-FIVE (continued)

Her foolish warring children keep
The grateful armistice of sleep.
For what tremendous errand's sake
Are we so blatantly awake?
What precious secret is our freight?
What king must be abroad so late?
Perhaps Death roams the hills to-night
And we rush forth to give him fight.
Or else, perhaps, we speed his way
To some remote unthinking prey.
Perhaps a woman writhes in pain
And listens—listens for the train!
The train, that like an angel sings,
The train, with healing on its wings.
Now "Hawthorne!" the conductor cries.
My neighbor starts and rubs his eyes.
He hurries yawning through the car
And steps out where the houses are.
This is the reason of our quest!
Not wantonly we break the rest
Of town and village, nor do we
Lightly profane night's sanctity.
What Love commands the train fulfills,

THE TWELVE-FORTY-FIVE (continued)

And beautiful upon the hills
Are these our feet of burnished steel.
Subtly and certainly I feel
That Glen Rock welcomes us to her
And silent Ridgewood seems to stir
And smile, because she knows the train
Has brought her children back again.
We carry people home—and so
God speeds us, wheresoe'er we go.
Hohokus, Waldwick, Allendale
Lift sleepy heads to give us hail.
In Ramsey, Mahwah, Suffern stand
Houses that wistfully demand
A father—son—some human thing
That this, the midnight train, may bring.
The trains that travel in the day
They hurry folks to work or play.
The midnight train is slow and old
But of it let this thing be told,
To its high honor be it said
It carries people home to bed.
My cottage lamp shines white and clear.
God bless the train that brought me here.

PENNIES

A FEW long-hoarded pennies in his hand
  Behold him stand;
A kilted Hedonist, perplexed and sad.
The joy that once he had,
The first delight of ownership is fled.
He bows his little head.
Ah, cruel Time, to kill
That splendid thrill!

Then in his tear-dimmed eyes
New lights arise.
He drops his treasured pennies on the ground,
They roll and bound
And scattered, rest.
Now with what zest
He runs to find his errant wealth again!

So unto men
Doth God, depriving that He may bestow.
Fame, health and money go,
But that they may, new found, be newly sweet.

PENNIES (continued)

Yea, at His feet
Sit, waiting us, to their concealment bid,
All they, our lovers, whom His Love hath hid.

Lo, comfort blooms on pain, and peace on strife,
    And gain on loss.
What is the key to Everlasting Life?
    A blood-stained Cross.

TREES

(For Mrs. Henry Mills Alden)

I THINK that I shall never see
  A poem lovely as a tree.

A tree whose hungry mouth is prest
Against the earth's sweet flowing breast;

A tree that looks at God all day,
And lifts her leafy arms to pray;

A tree that may in Summer wear
A nest of robins in her hair;

Upon whose bosom snow has lain;
Who intimately lives with rain.

Poems are made by fools like me,
But only God can make a tree.

(1914)

Joyce Kilmer

STARS

(For the Rev. James J. Daly, S. J.)

BRIGHT stars, yellow stars, flashing through
the air,
Are you errant strands of Lady Mary's hair?
As she slits the cloudy veil and bends down
through,
Do you fall across her cheeks and over heaven
too?

Gay stars, little stars, you are little eyes,
Eyes of baby angels playing in the skies.
Now and then a winged child turns his merry
face
Down toward the spinning world—what a funny
place!

Jesus Christ came from the Cross (Christ re-
ceive my soul!)
In each perfect hand and foot there was a bloody
hole.

STARS (continued)

Four great iron spikes there were, red and never
    dry,
Michael plucked them from the Cross and set
    them in the sky.

Christ's Troop, Mary's Guard, God's own men,
Draw your swords and strike at Hell and strike
    again.
Every steel-born spark that flies where God's
    battles are,
Flashes past the face of God, and is a star.

OLD POETS

(For Robert Cortez Holliday)

IF I should live in a forest
  And sleep underneath a tree,
No grove of impudent saplings
  Would make a home for me.

I'd go where the old oaks gather,
  Serene and good and strong,
And they would not sigh and tremble
  And vex me with a song.

The pleasantest sort of poet
  Is the poet who's old and wise,
With an old white beard and wrinkles
  About his kind old eyes.

For these young flippertigibbets
  A-rhyming their hours away
They won't be still like honest men
  And listen to what you say.

OLD POETS (continued)

The young poet screams forever
    About his sex and his soul;
But the old man listens, and smokes his pipe,
    And polishes its bowl.

There should be a club for poets
    Who have come to seventy year.
They should sit in a great hall drinking
    Red wine and golden beer.

They would shuffle in of an evening,
    Each one to his cushioned seat,
And there would be mellow talking
    And silence rich and sweet.

There is no peace to be taken
    With poets who are young,
For they worry about the wars to be fought
    And the songs that must be sung.

But the old man knows that he's in his chair
    And that God's on His throne in the sky.
So he sits by the fire in comfort
    And he lets the world spin by.

DELICATESSEN

WHY is that wanton gossip Fame
    So dumb about this man's affairs?
Why do we titter at his name
    Who come to buy his curious wares?

Here is a shop of wonderment.
    From every land has come a prize;
Rich spices from the Orient,
    And fruit that knew Italian skies,

And figs that ripened by the sea
    In Smyrna, nuts from hot Brazil,
Strange pungent meats from Germany,
    And currants from a Grecian hill.

He is the lord of goodly things
    That make the poor man's table gay,
Yet of his worth no minstrel sings
    And on his tomb there is no bay.

DELICATESSEN (continued)

Perhaps he lives and dies unpraised,
　　This trafficker in humble sweets,
Because his little shops are raised
　　By thousands in the city streets.

Yet stars in greater numbers shine,
　　And violets in millions grow,
And they in many a golden line
　　Are sung, as every child must know.

Perhaps Fame thinks his worried eyes,
　　His wrinkled, shrewd, pathetic face,
His shop, and all he sells and buys
　　Are desperately commonplace.

Well, it is true he has no sword
　　To dangle at his booted knees.
He leans across a slab of board,
　　And draws his knife and slices cheese.

He never heard of chivalry,
　　He longs for no heroic times;
He thinks of pickles, olives, tea,
　　And dollars, nickles, cents and dimes.

DELICATESSEN (continued)

His world has narrow walls, it seems;
    By counters is his soul confined;
His wares are all his hopes and dreams,
    They are the fabric of his mind.

Yet—in a room above the store
    There is a woman—and a child
Pattered just now across the floor;
    The shopman looked at him and smiled.

For, once he thrilled with high romance
    And tuned to love his eager voice.
Like any cavalier of France
    He wooed the maiden of his choice.

And now deep in his weary heart
    Are sacred flames that whitely burn.
He has of Heaven's grace a part
    Who loves, who is beloved in turn.

And when the long day's work is done,
    (How slow the leaden minutes ran!)
Home, with his wife and little son,
    He is no huckster, but a man!

DELICATESSEN (continued)

And there are those who grasp his hand,
  Who drink with him and wish him well.
O in no drear and lonely land
  Shall he who honors friendship dwell.

And in his little shop, who knows
  What bitter games of war are played?
Why, daily on each corner grows
  A foe to rob him of his trade.

He fights, and for his fireside's sake;
  He fights for clothing and for bread:
The lances of his foemen make
  A steely halo round his head.

He decks his window artfully,
  He haggles over paltry sums.
In this strange field his war must be
  And by such blows his triumph comes.

What if no trumpet sounds to call
  His armed legions to his side?
What if, to no ancestral hall
  He comes in all a victor's pride?

DELICATESSEN (continued)

The scene shall never fit the deed.
    Grotesquely wonders come to pass.
The fool shall mount an Arab steed
    And Jesus ride upon an ass.

This man has home and child and wife
    And battle set for every day.
This man has God and love and life;
    These stand, all else shall pass away.

O Carpenter of Nazareth,
    Whose mother was a village maid,
Shall we, Thy children, blow our breath
    In scorn on any humble trade?

Have pity on our foolishness
    And give us eyes, that we may see
Beneath the shopman's clumsy dress
    The splendor of humanity!

SERVANT GIRL AND GROCER'S BOY

HER lips' remark was: "Oh, you kid!"
Her soul spoke thus (I know it did):

"O king of realms of endless joy,
My own, my golden grocer's boy,

I am a princess forced to dwell
Within a lonely kitchen cell,

While you go dashing through the land
With loveliness on every hand.

Your whistle strikes my eager ears
Like music of the choiring spheres.

The mighty earth grows faint and reels
Beneath your thundering wagon wheels.

How keenly, perilously sweet
To cling upon that swaying seat!

SERVANT GIRL AND GROCER'S BOY (cont.)

How happy she who by your side
May share the splendors of that ride!

Ah, if you will not take my hand
And bear me off across the land,

Then, traveller from Arcady,
Remain awhile and comfort me.

What other maiden can you find
So young and delicate and kind?"

Her lips' remark was: "Oh, you kid!"
Her soul spoke thus (I know it did).

WEALTH

(For Aline)

FROM what old ballad, or from what rich
    frame
  Did you descend to glorify the earth?
Was it from Chaucer's singing book you came?
  Or did Watteau's small brushes give you birth?

Nothing so exquisite as that slight hand
  Could Raphael or Leonardo trace.
Nor could the poets know in Fairyland
  The changing wonder of your lyric face.

I would possess a host of lovely things,
  But I am poor and such joys may not be.
So God who lifts the poor and humbles kings
  Sent loveliness itself to dwell with me.

MARTIN

WHEN I am tired of earnest men,
    Intense and keen and sharp and clever,
Pursuing fame with brush or pen
    Or counting metal disks forever,
Then from the halls of Shadowland
    Beyond the trackless purple sea
Old Martin's ghost comes back to stand
    Beside my desk and talk to me.

Still on his delicate pale face
    A quizzical thin smile is showing,
His cheeks are wrinkled like fine lace,
    His kind blue eyes are gay and glowing.
He wears a brilliant-hued cravat,
    A suit to match his soft grey hair,
A rakish stick, a knowing hat,
    A manner blithe and debonair.

How good that he who always knew
    That being lovely was a duty,
Should have gold halls to wander through
    And should himself inhabit beauty.

MARTIN (continued)

How like his old unselfish way
  To leave those halls of splendid mirth
And comfort those condemned to stay
  Upon the dull and sombre earth.

Some people ask: "What cruel chance
  Made Martin's life so sad a story?"
Martin? Why, he exhaled romance,
  And wore an overcoat of glory.
A fleck of sunlight in the street,
  A horse, a book, a girl who smiled,
Such visions made each moment sweet
  For this receptive ancient child.

Because it was old Martin's lot
  To be, not make, a decoration,
Shall we then scorn him, having not
  His genius of appreciation?
Rich joy and love he got and gave;
  His heart was merry as his dress;
Pile laurel wreaths upon his grave
  Who did not gain, but was, success!

THE APARTMENT HOUSE

SEVERE against the pleasant arc of sky
    The great stone box is cruelly displayed.
    The street becomes more dreary from its
        shade,
And vagrant breezes touch its walls and die.
Here sullen convicts in their chains might lie,
    Or slaves toil dumbly at some dreary trade.
    How worse than folly is their labor made
Who cleft the rocks that this might rise on high!

Yet, as I look, I see a woman's face
    Gleam from a window far above the street.
This is a house of homes, a sacred place,
    By human passion made divinely sweet.
How all the building thrills with sudden grace
    Beneath the magic of Love's golden feet!

AS WINDS THAT BLOW AGAINST A STAR

(For Aline)

NOW by what whim of wanton chance
  Do radiant eyes know sombre days?
And feet that shod in light should dance
  Walk weary and laborious ways?

But rays from Heaven, white and whole,
  May penetrate the gloom of earth;
And tears but nourish, in your soul,
  The glory of celestial mirth.

The darts of toil and sorrow, sent
  Against your peaceful beauty, are
As foolish and as impotent
  As winds that blow against a star.

ST. LAURENCE

WITHIN the broken Vatican
    The murdered Pope is lying dead.
The soldiers of Valerian
   Their evil hands are wet and red.

Unarmed, unmoved, St. Laurence waits,
   His cassock is his only mail.
The troops of Hell have burst the gates,
   But Christ is Lord, He shall prevail.

They have encompassed him with steel,
   They spit upon his gentle face,
He smiles and bleeds, nor will reveal
   The Church's hidden treasure-place.

Ah, faithful steward, worthy knight,
   Well hast thou done.   Behold thy fee!
Since thou hast fought the goodly fight
   A martyr's death is fixed for thee.

ST. LAURENCE (continued)

St. Laurence, pray for us to bear
    The faith which glorifies thy name.
St. Laurence, pray for us to share
    The wounds of Love's consuming flame.

TO A YOUNG POET WHO KILLED
HIMSELF

WHEN you had played with life a space
        And made it drink and lust and sing,
You flung it back into God's face
    And thought you did a noble thing.
"Lo, I have lived and loved," you said,
    "And sung to fools too dull to hear me.
Now for a cool and grassy bed
    With violets in blossom near me."

Well, rest is good for weary feet,
    Although they ran for no great prize;
And violets are very sweet,
    Although their roots are in your eyes.
But hark to what the earthworms say
    Who share with you your muddy haven:
"The fight was on—you ran away.
    You are a coward and a craven.

"The rug is ruined where you bled;
    It was a dirty way to die!
To put a bullet through your head
    And make a silly woman cry!

TO A YOUNG POET WHO KILLED HIMSELF
(continued)

You could not vex the merry stars
   Nor make them heed you, dead or living.
Not all your puny anger mars
   God's irresistible forgiving.

"Yes, God forgives and men forget,
   And you're forgiven and forgotten.
You might be gaily sinning yet
   And quick and fresh instead of rotten.
And when you think of love and fame
   And all that might have come to pass,
Then don't you feel a little shame?
   And don't you think you were an ass?"

MEMORIAL DAY

"Dulce et decorum est"

THE bugle echoes shrill and sweet,
 But not of war it sings to-day.
The road is rhythmic with the feet
 Of men-at-arms who come to pray.

The roses blossom white and red
 On tombs where weary soldiers lie;
Flags wave above the honored dead
 And martial music cleaves the sky.

Above their wreath-strewn graves we kneel,
 They kept the faith and fought the fight.
Through flying lead and crimson steel
 They plunged for Freedom and the Right.

May we, their grateful children, learn
 Their strength, who lie beneath this sod,
Who went through fire and death to earn
 At last the accolade of God. -

MEMORIAL DAY (continued)

In shining rank on rank arrayed
   They march, the legions of the Lord;
He is their Captain unafraid,
   The Prince of Peace . . . Who brought a
     sword.

THE ROSARY

NOT on the lute, nor harp of many strings
    Shall all men praise the Master of all song.
  Our life is brief, one saith, and art is long;
And skilled must be the laureates of kings.
Silent, O lips that utter foolish things!
    Rest, awkward fingers striking all notes wrong!
    How from your toil shall issue, white and
      strong,
Music like that God's chosen poet sings?

There is one harp that any hand can play,
    And from its strings what harmonies arise!
There is one song that any mouth can say,—
    A song that lingers when all singing dies.
When on their beads our Mother's children pray
    Immortal music charms the grateful skies.

VISION

(For Aline)

HOMER, they tell us, was blind and could
    not see the beautiful faces
  Looking up into his own and reflecting the joy
    of his dream,
  Yet did he seem
Gifted with eyes that could follow the gods to
    their holiest places.

I have no vision of gods, not of Eros with love-
    arrows laden,
  Jupiter thundering death or of Juno his white-
    breasted queen,
  Yet have I seen
All of the joy of the world in the innocent heart
    of a maiden.

TO CERTAIN POETS

NOW is the rhymer's honest trade
A thing for scornful laughter made.

The merchant's sneer, the clerk's disdain,
These are the burden of our pain.

Because of you did this befall,
You brought this shame upon us all.

You little poets mincing there
With women's hearts and women's hair!

How sick Dan Chaucer's ghost must be
To hear you lisp of "Poesie"!

A heavy-handed blow, I think,
Would make your veins drip scented ink.

You strut and smirk your little while
So mildly, delicately vile!

TO CERTAIN POETS (continued)

Your tiny voices mock God's wrath,
You snails that crawl along His path!

Why, what has God or man to do
With wet, amorphous things like you?

This thing alone you have achieved:
Because of you, it is believed

That all who earn their bread by rhyme
Are like yourselves, exuding slime.

Oh, cease to write, for very shame,
Ere all men spit upon our name!

Take up your needles, drop your pen,
And leave the poet's craft to men!

LOVE'S LANTERN

(For Aline)

BECAUSE the road was steep and long
    And through a dark and lonely land,
God set upon my lips a song
    And put a lantern in my hand.

Through miles on weary miles of night
    That stretch relentless in my way
My lantern burns serene and white,
    An unexhausted cup of day.

O golden lights and lights like wine,
    How dim your boasted splendors are.
Behold this little lamp of mine;
    It is more starlike than a star!

ST. ALEXIS

Patron of Beggars

WE who beg for bread as we daily tread
  Country lane and city street,
Let us kneel and pray on the broad highway
  To the saint with the vagrant feet.
Our altar light is a buttercup bright,
  And our shrine is a bank of sod,
But still we share St. Alexis' care,
  The Vagabond of God.

They gave him a home in purple Rome
  And a princess for his bride,
But he rowed away on his wedding day
  Down the Tiber's rushing tide.
And he came to land on the Asian strand
  Where the heathen people dwell;
As a beggar he strayed and he preached and
      prayed
  And he saved their souls from hell.

ST. ALEXIS (continued)

Bowed with years and pain he came back again
    To his father's dwelling place.
There was none to see who this tramp might be,
    For they knew not his bearded face.
But his father said, "Give him drink and bread
    And a couch underneath the stair."
So Alexis crept to his hole and slept.
    But he might not linger there.

For when night came down on the seven-hilled
        town,
    And the emperor hurried in,
Saying, "Lo, I hear that a saint is near
    Who will cleanse us of our sin,"
Then they looked in vain where the saint had lain,
    For his soul had fled afar,
From his fleshly home he had gone to roam
    Where the gold-paved highways are.

We who beg for bread as we daily tread
    Country lane and city street,
Let us kneel and pray on the broad highway
    To the saint with the vagrant feet.

ST. ALEXIS (continued)

Our altar light is a buttercup bright,
   And our shrine is a bank of sod,
But still we share St. Alexis' care,
   The Vagabond of God!

FOLLY

(For A. K. K.)

WHAT distant mountains thrill and glow
  Beneath our Lady Folly's tread?
Why has she left us, wise in woe,
 Shrewd, practical, uncomforted?
We cannot love or dream or sing,
 We are too cynical to pray,
There is no joy in anything
 Since Lady Folly went away.

Many a knight and gentle maid,
 Whose glory shines from years gone by,
Through ignorance was unafraid
 And as a fool knew how to die.
Saint Folly rode beside Jehanne
 And broke the ranks of Hell with her,
And Folly's smile shone brightly on
 Christ's plaything, Brother Juniper.

Our minds are troubled and defiled
 By study in a weary school.

FOLLY (continued)

O for the folly of the child!
  The ready courage of the fool!
Lord, crush our knowledge utterly
  And make us humble, simple men;
And cleansed of wisdom, let us see
  Our Lady Folly's face again.

MADNESS

(For Sara Teasdale)

THE lonely farm, the crowded street,
 The palace and the slum,
Give welcome to my silent feet
 As, bearing gifts, I come.

Last night a beggar crouched alone,
 A ragged helpless thing;
I set him on a moonbeam throne—
 Today he is a king.

Last night a king in orb and crown
 Held court with splendid cheer;
Today he tears his purple gown
 And moans and shrieks in fear.

Not iron bars, nor flashing spears,
 Not land, nor sky, nor sea,
Nor love's artillery of tears
 Can keep mine own from me.

MADNESS (continued)

Serene, unchanging, ever fair,
   I smile with secret mirth
And in a net of mine own hair
   I swing the captive earth.

POETS

VAIN is the chiming of forgotten bells
    That the wind sways above a ruined
      shrine.
Vainer his voice in whom no longer dwells
   Hunger that craves immortal Bread and Wine.

Light songs we breathe that perish with our
    breath
  Out of our lips that have not kissed the rod.
They shall not live who have not tasted death.
   They only sing who are struck dumb by God.

CITIZEN OF THE WORLD

No longer of Him be it said
    "He hath no place to lay His head."

In every land a constant lamp
Flames by His small and mighty camp.

There is no strange and distant place
That is not gladdened by His face.

And every nation kneels to hail
The Splendour shining through Its veil.

Cloistered beside the shouting street,
Silent, He calls me to His feet.

Imprisoned for His love of me
He makes my spirit greatly free.

And through my lips that uttered sin
The King of Glory enters in.

TO A BLACKBIRD AND HIS MATE
WHO DIED IN THE SPRING

(For Kenton)

AN iron hand has stilled the throats
    That throbbed with loud and rhythmic glee
And dammed the flood of silver notes
    That drenched the world in melody.
The blosmy apple boughs are yearning
For their wild choristers' returning,
    But no swift wings flash through the tree.

Ye that were glad and fleet and strong,
    Shall Silence take you in her net?
And shall Death quell that radiant song
    Whose echo thrills the meadow yet?
Burst the frail web about you clinging
And charm Death's cruel heart with singing
    Till with strange tears his eyes are wet.

The scented morning of the year
    Is old and stale now ye are gone.
No friendly songs the children hear
    Among the bushes on the lawn.

TO A BLACKBIRD AND HIS MATE WHO
DIED IN THE SPRING (continued)

When babies wander out a-Maying
Will ye, their bards, afar be straying?
   Unhymned by you, what is the dawn?

Nay, since ye loved ye cannot die.
   Above the stars is set your nest.
Through Heaven's fields ye sing and fly
   And in the trees of Heaven rest.
And little children in their dreaming
Shall see your soft black plumage gleaming
   And smile, by your clear music blest.

THE FOURTH SHEPHERD

(For Thomas Walsh)

I

ON nights like this the huddled sheep
    Are like white clouds upon the grass,
And merry herdsmen guard their sleep
    And chat and watch the big stars pass.

It is a pleasant thing to lie
    Upon the meadow on the hill
With kindly fellowship near by
    Of sheep and men of gentle will.

I lean upon my broken crook
    And dream of sheep and grass and men—
O shameful eyes that cannot look
    On any honest thing again!

On bloody feet I clambered down
    And fled the wages of my sin,
I am the leavings of the town,
    And meanly serve its meanest inn.

THE FOURTH SHEPHERD (continued)

I tramp the courtyard stones in grief,
 While sleep takes man and beast to her.
And every cloud is calling "Thief!"
 And every star calls "Murderer!"

THE FOURTH SHEPHERD (continued)

II

The hand of God is sure and strong,
    Nor shall a man forever flee
The bitter punishment of wrong.
    The wrath of God is over me!

With ashen bread and wine of tears
    Shall I be solaced in my pain.
I wear through black and endless years
    Upon my brow the mark of Cain.

THE FOURTH SHEPHERD (continued)

III

Poor vagabond, so old and mild,
  Will they not keep him for a night?
And She, a woman great with child,
  So frail and pitiful and white.

Good people, since the tavern door
  Is shut to you, come here instead.
See, I have cleansed my stable floor
  And piled fresh hay to make a bed.

Here is some milk and oaten cake.
  Lie down and sleep and rest you fair,
Nor fear, O simple folk, to take
  The bounty of a child of care.

THE FOURTH SHEPHERD (continued)

IV

On nights like this the huddled sheep—
   I never saw a night so fair.
How huge the sky is, and how deep!
   And how the planets flash and glare!

At dawn beside my drowsy flock
   What wingéd music I have heard!
But now the clouds with singing rock
   As if the sky were turning bird.

O blinding Light, O blinding Light!
   Burn through my heart with sweetest pain.
O flaming Song, most loudly bright,
   Consume away my deadly stain!

THE FOURTH SHEPHERD (continued)

V

The stable glows against the sky,
   And who are these that throng the way?
My three old comrades hasten by
   And shining angels kneel and pray.

The door swings wide—I cannot go—
   I must and yet I dare not see.
Lord, who am I that I should know—
   Lord, God, be merciful to me!

THE FOURTH SHEPHERD (continued)

VI

O Whiteness, whiter than the fleece
  Of new-washed sheep on April sod!
O Breath of Life, O Prince of Peace,
  O Lamb of God, O Lamb of God!

EASTER

THE air is like a butterfly
    With frail blue wings.
The happy earth looks at the sky
    And sings.

MOUNT HOUVENKOPF

SERENE he stands, with mist serenely
    crowned,
  And draws a cloak of trees about his breast.
  The thunder roars but cannot break his rest
And from his rugged face the tempests bound.
He does not heed the angry lightning's wound,
  The raging blizzard is his harmless guest,
  And human life is but a passing jest
To him who sees Time spin the years around.

But fragile souls, in skyey reaches find
  High vantage-points and view him from afar.
How low he seems to the ascended mind,
  How brief he seems where all things endless
      are;
This little playmate of the mighty wind
  This young companion of an ancient star.

THE HOUSE WITH NOBODY IN IT

WHENEVER I walk to Suffern along the
    Erie track
I go by a poor old farmhouse with its shingles
    broken and black.
I suppose I've passed it a hundred times, but I
    always stop for a minute
And look at the house, the tragic house, the
    house with nobody in it.

I never have seen a haunted house, but I hear
    there are such things;
That they hold the talk of spirits, their mirth
    and sorrowings.
I know this house isn't haunted, and I wish it
    were, I do;
For it wouldn't be so lonely if it had a ghost or
    two.

This house on the road to Suffern needs a dozen
    panes of glass,
And somebody ought to weed the walk and take
    a scythe to the grass.

THE HOUSE WITH NOBODY IN IT (cont.)

It needs new paint and shingles, and the vines
    should be trimmed and tied;
But what it needs the most of all is some people
    living inside.

If I had a lot of money and all my debts were
    paid
I'd put a gang of men to work with brush and
    saw and spade.
I'd buy that place and fix it up the way it used
    to be
And I'd find some people who wanted a home and
    give it to them free.

Now, a new house standing empty, with staring
    window and door,
Looks idle, perhaps, and foolish, like a hat on
    its block in the store.
But there's nothing mournful about it; it can-
    not be sad and lone
For the lack of something within it that it has
    never known.

THE HOUSE WITH NOBODY IN IT (cont.)

But a house that has done what a house should
     do, a house that has sheltered life,
That has put its loving wooden arms around a
     man and his wife,
A house that has echoed a baby's laugh and held
     up his stumbling feet,
Is the saddest sight, when it's left alone, that ever
     your eyes could meet.

So whenever I go to Suffern along the Erie track
I never go by the empty house without stopping
     and looking back,
Yet it hurts me to look at the crumbling roof
     and the shutters fallen apart,
For I can't help thinking the poor old house is
     a house with a broken heart.

DAVE LILLY

THERE'S a brook on the side of Greylock
    that used to be full of trout,
But there's nothing there now but minnows;
    they say it is all fished out.
I fished there many a Summer day some twenty
    years ago,
And I never quit without getting a mess of a
    dozen or so.

There was a man, Dave Lilly, who lived on the
    North Adams road,
And he spent all his time fishing, while his neigh-
    bors reaped and sowed.
He was the luckiest fisherman in the Berkshire
    hills, I think.
And when he didn't go fishing he'd sit in the
    tavern and drink.

Well, Dave is dead and buried and nobody cares
    very much;
They have no use in Greylock for drunkards and
    loafers and such.

DAVE LILLY (continued)

But I always liked Dave Lilly, he was pleasant
    as you could wish;
He was shiftless and good-for-nothing, but he
    certainly could fish.

The other night I was walking up the hill from
    Williamstown
And I came to the brook I mentioned, and I
    stopped on the bridge and sat down.
I looked at the blackened water with its little
    flecks of white
And I heard it ripple and whisper in the still of
    the Summer night.

And after I'd been there a minute it seemed to
    me I could feel
The presence of someone near me, and I heard
    the hum of a reel.
And the water was churned and broken, and
    something was brought to land
By a twist and flirt of a shadowy rod in a deft
    and shadowy hand.

DAVE LILLY (continued)

I scrambled down to the brookside and hunted
    all about;
There wasn't a sign of a fisherman; there wasn't
    a sign of a trout.
But I heard somebody chuckle behind the hol-
    low oak
And I got a whiff of tobacco like Lilly used to
    smoke.

It's fifteen years, they tell me, since anyone fished
    that brook;
And there's nothing in it but minnows that nib-
    ble the bait off your hook.
But before the sun has risen and after the moon
    has set
I know that it's full of ghostly trout for Lilly's
    ghost to get.

I guess I'll go to the tavern and get a bottle of
    rye
And leave it down by the hollow oak, where
    Lilly's ghost went by.

DAVE LILLY (continued)

I meant to go up on the hillside and try to find
    his grave
And put some flowers on it—but this will be bet-
    ter for Dave.

ALARM CLOCKS

WHEN Dawn strides out to wake a dewy
farm
  Across green fields and yellow hills of hay
    The little twittering birds laugh in his way
And poise triumphant on his shining arm.
He bears a sword of flame but not to harm
    The wakened life that feels his quickening
      sway
    And barnyard voices shrilling "It is day!"
Take by his grace a new and alien charm.

But in the city, like a wounded thing
    That limps to cover from the angry chase,
He steals down streets where sickly arc-lights
      sing,
    And wanly mock his young and shameful face;
And tiny gongs with cruel fervor ring
    In many a high and dreary sleeping place.

WAVERLEY

1814-1914

WHEN, on a novel's newly printed page
    We find a maudlin eulogy of sin,
    And read of ways that harlots wander in,
And of sick souls that writhe in helpless rage;
Or when Romance, bespectacled and sage,
    Taps on her desk and bids the class begin
    To con the problems that have always been
Perplexed mankind's unhappy heritage;

Then in what robes of honor habited
    The laureled wizard of the North appears!
Who raised Prince Charlie's cohorts from the
        dead,
    Made Rose's mirth and Flora's noble tears,
And formed that shining legion at whose head
    Rides Waverley, triumphant o'er the years!